A
CHILD'S
RIGHT
TO
RIGHTS

United Nations

Acknowledgements

With thanks to Jennifer Arena for writing the texts and to Cécile Carlier and Rhéal LeBlanc of the United Nations Information Service in Geneva and Victor Fernandez of the Office of the United Nations High Commissioner for Human Rights (OHCHR) for their assistance in providing the illustrations.

Note about the illustrations

The illustrations selected for this book were some of the winners of an international drawing competition titled "Kids for Human Rights" which celebrated the 70th anniversary of the Universal Declaration of Human Rights. Organized by the United Nations Information Service in Geneva, the Gabarron Foundation and the Office of the High Commissioner for Human Rights, the competition attracted more than 17,000 entries from children between the ages of 10 and 14 from 71 countries around the world. Children were asked to draw or paint pictures in three categories: the first showing the human right they felt most strongly about defending, the second one showing a human rights defender they admired, or the third, showing how they could personally defend or promote human rights. To learn more, visit kids4humanrights.org.

I am a kid, and I have rights!

In 1989, the countries that belonged to the United Nations got together and, for the first time ever, wrote down what rights children have, fifty-four rights in all. From the right to play to the right to learn to the right to a name—the United Nations thought of everything!

This meeting was called the Convention of the Rights of the Child. It's made a big difference in the way children around the world are treated every day.

As you read this book, you'll learn about most of these rights. Each one is very important. Together, these rights help you and me and children everywhere live healthy and happy lives!

I have many special rights, and they protect me, until I turn eighteen years old and become an adult. All children, like me, everywhere around the world, have these rights.

What is a right? It's something that I can claim, something that belongs to me and can't be taken away.

ARTICLE 1   Definition of a Child

I have the right to be treated fairly. If I'm treated differently because of what I look like, where I live, the language I speak, or because of my gender, that's not okay!

I always try to treat people with respect—they should treat me the same way. It's only fair.

ARTICLE 2 No Discrimination

Artist
Bianca Linheiro, 12, Portugal

Adults make a lot of decisions.
When they do, they need to think about
how I will be as safe and happy as possible.
If governments and other groups make
choices that involve my rights, they have to
do what's best for me!

ARTICLE 3   Best Interests of the Child

I have the right to live and survive and grow up healthy. The government of my country should make sure all my rights are protected. That way I can become the best person I can be!

ARTICLE 5 Life, Survival and Development

Artist
Laura Ferros de Azevedo, 14, Portugal
This illustration was initially intended for Article 2 of the Universal Declaration of Human Rights.

ACE POWER |COL UR POWER|GENDER POWER|LANGUAGE POWER|RELIGION POWE
NO
uman
Is
LLEGAL
Human Power
LOVE is LOVE
ALL EQUAL
ALL DIFERENT
freedom power
justice FOREVER
We All CAN DO It!
Article 2
All lives mater.
liberty FOREVER
Freedom OF Choice
Equality power

I have the right to belong to my country or nation, just like adults do. It's called my nationality. Plus I have the right to know who my parents are and to be cared for by them. That's a whole lot of rights, right there!

ARTICLE 6   Name and Nationality
ARTICLE 7   Identity

Artist
Rocío Bugueño López, 14, Chile

I have the right to live with my parents. If my parents don't live together, if they're divorced or separated, I have the right to be in contact with both of them.

ARTICLE 9   Keeping Families Together

Artist
Fiorenza Beretta Musiris, 13, Peru

What about if my parents live in different countries? I can move between the countries. These are my rights, but **ONLY** if it's good for me. If it might hurt me, then I don't have to either live with my parents or stay in touch. **My safety is important.**

ARTICLE 10   Contact with Parents Across Countries

Artist
Loulwa Fakhoury, 12, Lebanon

LouLu
Fakih
30 / 10 / 2018

My opinion matters! I have the right to say what I think when someone is making a decision about me. People have to listen to and consider what I say.

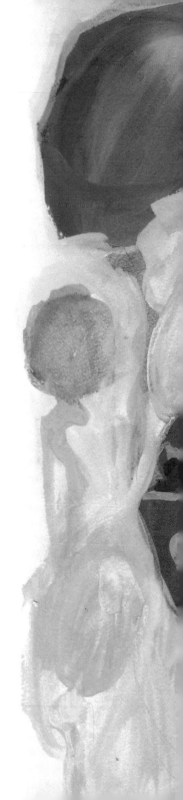

ARTICLE 12   Respect for Children's Views

Artist
Masha Erohina, 10, Russia

I can share my thoughts any way I want—I can say them, write them, or even draw them. That doesn't mean I can tell adults what to do. Too bad, because there are lots of things I would change!

ARTICLE 13   Sharing Thoughts Freely

Artist
Marian Altuzar Castrejó, 13, Mexico

I can think what I want and believe what I want, as long as my beliefs don't keep other people from thinking or believing what they want. I can question what I learn, too.

Asking questions is an important part of growing up. Don't you think so?

ARTICLE 14   Freedom of Thought and Religion

Artist
Madie Crawshaw, 14, Australia

WE

ARE

SILENCED

FOR

OUR

DIFFERENT

BELIEFS

OR

OPINIONS

WHEN IT IS A HUMAN
RIGHT

I can choose my own friends, meet up with other children, and join or set up clubs and groups. I have the right to privacy— shhh, don't tell. And I have the right to get information that's important to me from the radio or newspaper, my computer . . . or from children's books like this one!

Artist
Macarena Diaz, 10, Bolivia

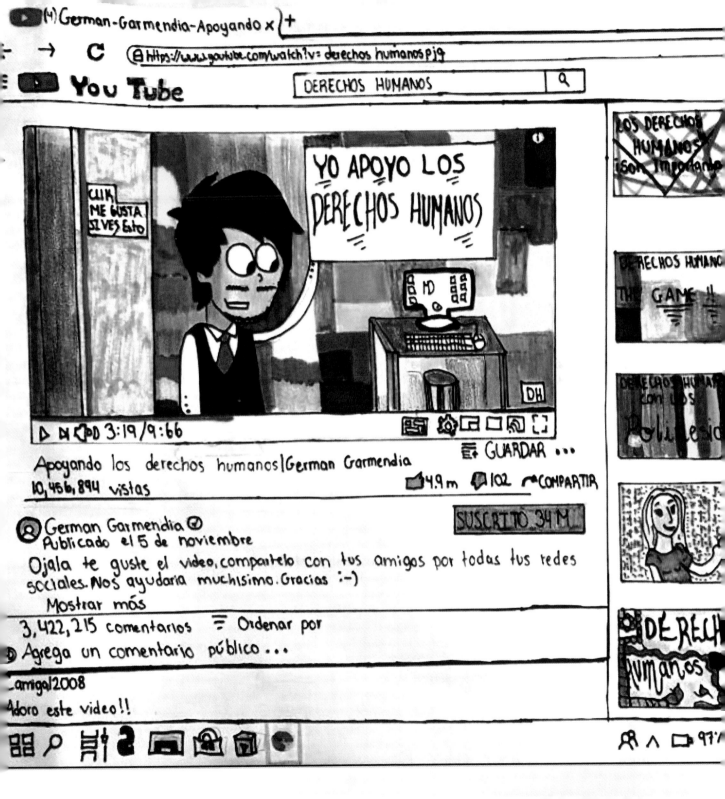

My parents share responsibility in bringing me up. If both my parents work away from our house and can't stay home with me, our government should offer services that make it easier for them to take care of me.

ARTICLE 18   Responsibility of Parents

Artist
Anastasiya Kazanceva, 11, Kazakhstan

I have the right to be safe. No one should hurt me or treat me badly. Not even my parents!

Sometimes when I do something wrong, my parents might punish me. They know how to teach me right from wrong without hurting me.

ARTICLE 19 Protection From Violence

Artist
Mona Jarekji, 12, Lebanon

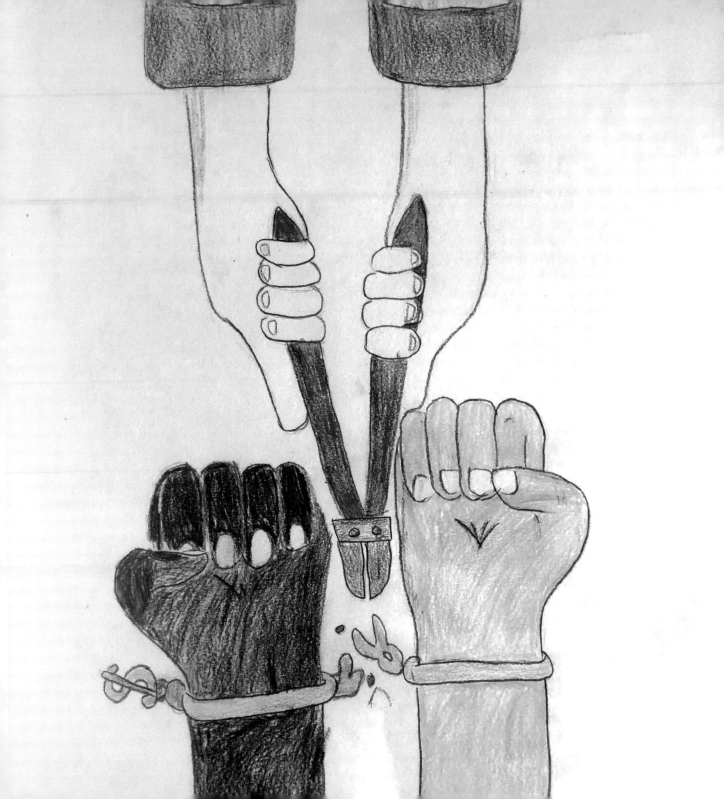

If my parents can't look after me,
I have the right to be taken care of by
someone who respects my religion,
my language, and my culture.

ARTICLE 20 Children without Families

Artist
Madeleine Yeh, 14, USA

Some children get adopted. Some children have to go into foster care. They have the same exact rights, even if they are taken to live in a different country!

ARTICLE 21   Children who are Adopted

Artist
Kostadinka Kostova, 10, Bulgaria

Sometimes children have to leave their homes because it's too dangerous, because of a natural disaster like a hurricane or an earthquake, or because of war. They might even have to go live in another country. These children are special. They are called refugees. If this happens to me, I have the right to special protection and help.

ARTICLE 22 Refugee Children

Artist
Antonio V Marques Tavares Tonico, 10, Brazil

Some children have disabilities. Maybe their brains aren't the same as other children's or maybe their bodies aren't. These children are awesome, too, and have the right to special care so they can lead full lives.

ARTICLE 23   Children with Disabilities

Artist
Avin Zamanifard, 12, Iran

nous sommes
different.

Chaque peau
à une qualité!

être riche neveux
pas dire conait
les meilleurs!

trois doigts
de moins et alors!
On peux encore
vivre.

une jambe
te moins. Ben
se nais pas grave!

Loi, Avin Zamanifard

Être moche ne veux
pas dire que tues moche!
(nul)

Être pauvre ça fait quoi?
Parce que elle est pauvre
sa ve dire quelle est
méchante?!?!?

une petite taille
ne dit pas que tu sais
à rien!

N'arceler pas les personne.
pour leurs apparence.
Parce que senais pas
eux qui ont choisi!

Safe water, good food, a clean place to live—I have the right to all these things! They are important because they help keep me healthy. They're so important that if people other than my parents is looking after me, someone has to check in to make sure I'm well taken care of.

ARTICLE 24 Health, Water, Food, Environment
ARTICLE 25 Review of A Child's Placement

Artist
Carolina Lerchundi Girardelli, 11, Argentina

If my family is poor, the government of our country should help us with food and clothes and a place to live. These are basic things that ALL children have a right to.

ARTICLE 26   Social and Economic Help
ARTICLE 27   Food, Clothing, a Safe Home

Artist
Raghad Al Khatib, 10, Qatar

The Earth Provides Enough
Resources For Every Man,

Woman And child To Live

comfortably

However, There Are People

In Power That choose To

Hoard It All

I have the right to learn! My school should be free and run in an orderly way. It should teach me how to live peacefully and respect other people. It should help me develop my talents. I have the right to get to highest education that I can—high school, college . . . or, hey, maybe I'll become a doctor!

ARTICLE 28 Access to Education
ARTICLE 29 Aims of Education

Artist
Bissan Iskandar, 11, Qatar

I have the right to learn about my culture. That's great, because my culture is super cool! I can learn and practice my own language and religion, too, whether lots of people in my country share them . . . or not many at all!

ARTICLE 30 Minority Culture, Language And Religion

Artist
Teodor Todorov, 12, Bulgaria

Now for one of my favorite rights—the right to play! Yes, I have that right, too, to play and relax. That can mean anything from painting to practicing football with my friends to reading or playing on the computer or flying a kite.

What's your favorite way to play?

ARTICLE 31   Rest, Play, Culture, Arts

Artist
Hanna Peresztegi, 13, Hungary

The government of my country needs to protect me from working in ways that aren't good for me. If the work makes me sick or hurts me, or if it keeps me from school and learning, then the government should step in.

Of course, that doesn't mean I don't have to do my chores!

ARTICLE 32   Protection from Harmful Work

Artist
João Marques, 13, Portugal

My body belongs to me, and no one can hurt me. No one should touch me in ways that make me feel unsafe, uncomfortable, or sad. My health is important. My safety is important. The government has to be watchful at all times to make sure no one does any of these things to me. I feel happy knowing that, don't you?

ARTICLE 34   Protection from Sexual Abuse
ARTICLE 35   Prevention of Sale and Trafficking
ARTICLE 36   Protection From Exploitation

Artist
Saied Muhammad Saleh, 12, Bangladesh

Wars happen—they're not good for anyone, especially not for children. Children who are younger than fifteen years old should never have to fight in a war. And for children who have been harmed or neglected? Governments should work hard to help them. I need my dignity. I need my self-respect. And I need my health.

ARTICLE 38 Protection in War
ARTICLE 39 Recovery and Reintegration

Artist
Eric Schliemann, 12, Brazil

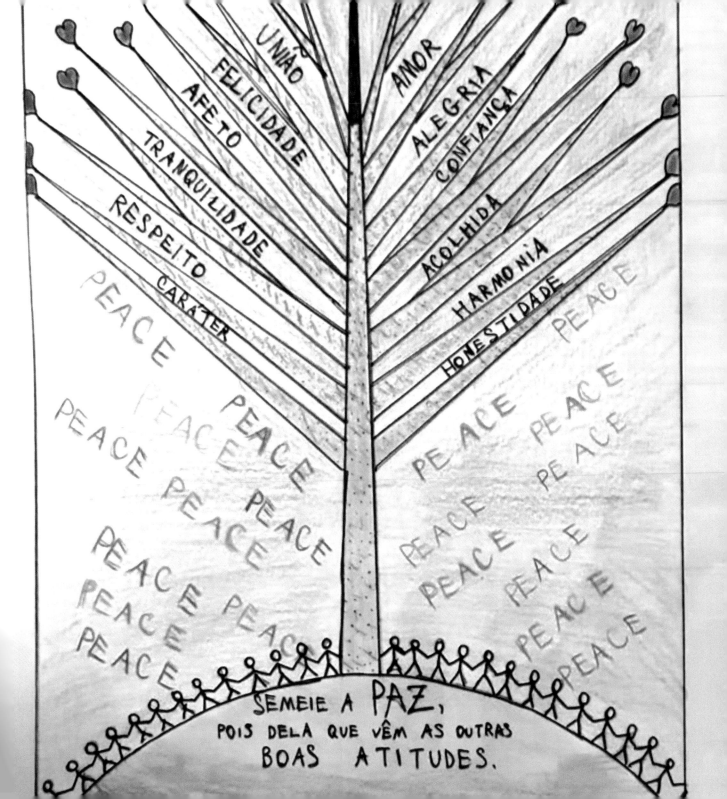

WANT TO LEARN MORE?

What is the United Nations?

The United Nations (UN) is an organization that brings countries to work together. It's a place where countries can meet to discuss the world's most difficult problems, like conflicts and war. In addition to keeping international peace and security, the UN protects human rights (which includes the children's rights in this book), delivers humanitarian aid to people in need, promotes sustainable development to protect our planet and upholds international law for a fair society for all.

The idea of the UN was born during World War II. World leaders wanted to find a way that would help bring peace for future generations. They realized that this was possible only if all nations worked together through a global organization. The UN was established on 24 October 1945 to be that organization. When it was founded, the UN had 51 Member States; there are now 193.

The goals of the United Nations are:
- to keep world peace
- to help countries get along
- to improve living conditions for people all over the world
- and to make the world a better place.

CONVENTION ON THE RIGHTS OF THE CHILD

The United Nations Convention on the Rights of the Child is an important agreement by countries who have promised to protect children's rights.

The Convention on the Rights of the Child explains who children are, all their rights, and the responsibilities of governments.

All the rights are connected, they are all equally important and they cannot be taken away from children.

If you want to learn more about the Convention of the Rights of the Child, go to www.unicef.org/child-rights-convention

A child is any person under the age of 18.

DEFINITION OF A CHILD

 All children have all these rights, no matter who they are, where they live, what language they speak, what their religion is, what they think, what they look like, if they are a boy or girl, if they have a disability, if they are rich or poor, and no matter who their parents or families are or what their parents or families believe or do. No child should be treated unfairly for any reason.

NO DISCRIMINATION

 When adults make decisions, they should think about how their decisions will affect children. All adults should do what is best for children. Governments should make sure children are protected and looked after by their parents, or by other people when this is needed. Governments should make sure that people and places responsible for looking after children are doing a good job.

BEST INTERESTS OF THE CHILD

 Governments must do all they can to make sure that every child in their countries can enjoy all the rights in this Convention.

MAKING RIGHTS REAL

 Governments should let families and communities guide their children so that, as they grow up, they learn to use their rights in the best way. The more children grow, the less guidance they will need.

FAMILY GUIDANCE AS CHILDREN DEVELOP

 Every child has the right to be alive. Governments must make sure that children survive and develop in the best possible way.

LIFE, SURVIVAL AND DEVELOPMENT

 Children must be registered when they are born and given a name which is officially recognized by the government. Children must have a nationality (belong to a country). Whenever possible, children should know their parents and be looked after by them.

NAME AND NATIONALITY

 Children have the right to their own identity – an official record of who they are which includes their name, nationality and family relations. No one should take this away from them, but if this happens, governments must help children to quickly get their identity back.

IDENTITY

 Children should not be separated from their parents unless they are not being properly looked after – for example, if a parent hurts or does not take care of a child. Children whose parents don't live together should stay in contact with both parents unless this might harm the child.

KEEPING FAMILIES TOGETHER

 If a child lives in a different country than their parents, governments must let the child and parents travel so that they can stay in contact and be together.

CONTACT WITH PARENTS ACROSS COUNTRIES

 Governments must stop children being taken out of the country when this is against the law – for example, being kidnapped by someone or held abroad by a parent when the other parent does not agree.

PROTECTION FROM KIDNAPPING

 Children have the right to give their opinions freely on issues that affect them. Adults should listen and take children seriously.

RESPECT FOR CHILDREN'S VIEWS

 Children have the right to give their opinions freely on issues that affect them. Adults should listen and take children seriously.

SHARING THOUGHTS FREELY

 Children can choose their own thoughts, opinions and religion, but this should not stop other people from enjoying their rights. Parents can guide children so that as they grow up, they learn to properly use this right.

FREEDOM OF THOUGHT AND RELIGION

 Children can join or set up groups or organisations, and they can meet with others, as long as this does not harm other people.

SETTING UP OR JOINING GROUPS

 Every child has the right to privacy. The law must protect children's privacy, family, home, communications and reputation (or good name) from any attack.

PROTECTION OF PRIVACY

 Children have the right to get information from the Internet, radio, television, newspapers, books and other sources. Adults should make sure the information they are getting is not harmful. Governments should encourage the media to share information from lots of different sources, in languages that all children can understand.

ACCESS TO INFORMATION

 Parents are the main people responsible for bringing up a child. When the child does not have any parents, another adult will have this responsibility and they are called a "guardian." Parents and guardians should always consider what is best for that child. Governments should help them. Where a child has both parents, both of them should be responsible for bringing up the child.

RESPONSIBILITY OF PARENTS

 Governments must protect children from violence, abuse and being neglected by anyone who looks after them.

PROTECTION FROM VIOLENCE

 Every child who cannot be looked after by their own family has the right to be looked after properly by people who respect the child's religion, culture, language and other aspects of their life.

CHILDREN WITHOUT FAMILIES

 When children are adopted, the most important thing is to do what is best for them. If a child cannot be properly looked after in their own country – for example by living with another family – then they might be adopted in another country.

CHILDREN WHO ARE ADOPTED